THANKSGIVING ACTIVITY BOOK

Check out our other books on Amazon

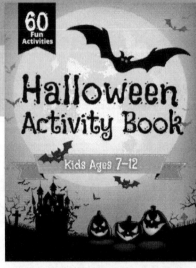

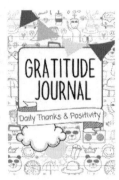

Share Your Feedback and Help Us Foster Creativity!
We value your input and encourage you to provide us with your thoughts.
Take a moment to visit Amazon and leave an honest review,
so we can continue to improve our service.
Thank you for your support!

Inside You Will Find

Word Search Puzzles

Crossword Puzzles

Mazes

Word Scrambles

Sudoku (123 & ABC)

Cryptograms

Double Word Puzzles

tic-tac-toe

Draw the Other Half

Copy the Picture

Coloring

Story Starters

Jokes

Would You Rather?

Word Search #1

Autumn Colors

```
M R H G Q S M Q G V E A F O O Q A Q P E
U P M A R O O N N Z P H L A E H N K P Q
R W M A H O G A N Y L H R T T U K X W M
R C O L I V E O U B E E Q S I E N N A W
X T T J P U R C R E K H Y I X Q L I O E
F G G I L B G E S A J M P T Y V I W Y G
K B Q Z U I P O A Q T R U W J T K M V D
K N F C M P F Q L M J P N S O C H R E M
J R K R O R V B D D B O N D T U T N U F
R F E C W Y T D H Q S E J D D A K X P M
F U A X N L B T N M Q Z R D D J R K M R
D H S W X R O I I S X A O Q T C L D Z O
N T A S Z H K R R V V T W J G Q M S G P
B T X O E P C H B U O H L E V N A K V F
N I E E M T Y D L C S K D C T I U U B U
A N S U Y I J G A Z O T M I R V V M H V
K R P X T E R R A C O T T A J W E J A R
Q S I Q G U C F L B S J S B D K O F M B
G M V G I S C A R L E T W W Y K C B K F
B U R N T O R A N G E T R Z O U S Y Q Y
```

AMBER	BRONZE	BURNT ORANGE
COPPER	CRIMSON	GOLD
MAHOGANY	MAROON	MAUVE
MUSTARD	OCHRE	OLIVE
PLUM	PUMPKIN	RUSSET
RUST	SCARLET	SIENNA
TAWNY	TERRACOTTA	

Maze #1

Crossword #1

Across

[6] The wooden figure used to scare away birds from crops

[7] The season during which Thanksgiving is celebrated

[8] Brave people who sailed on a big ship called the Mayflower to a new land a long time ago, and they celebrated the first Thanksgiving with Native Americans

[10] The orange gourd often carved into jack-o'-lanterns for Halloween

Down

[1] A tasty yellow vegetable with sweet kernels on a cob

[2] Having a lot of good things

[3] The dish made from bread and vegetables that's stuffed inside the turkey

[4] a bright and cheerful color, like the color of pumpkins and leaves in the fall, and it's often associated with autumn

[5] People who love and care for you, like your parents, siblings, and relatives

[9] Was a friendly Native American who helped the Pilgrims by teaching them how to plant crops and survive in their new home

Copy the Picture

Use the grid to copy the picture.
Copying one square at a time might be easier.
Be careful when counting the squares!

thanksgiving Story Starter

Complete the thanksgiving story!

"Dad, are you sure this time machine of yours is going to work?" I asked, peering skeptically at the contraption of blinking lights and whirring gears in our backyard. My father, sporting his trademark lab coat and a mischievous grin, adjusted his safety goggles and replied, "Well, there's only one way to find out, isn't there?" Before I could protest further, he hit a button, and with a cacophony of zaps and whirls, our entire family, along with our trusty dog, found ourselves hurtling through time, right into the heart of the very first thanksgiving.

tic-tac-toe

Player _____   Player _____

Score _____   Score _____

Word Scramble #1

Let's unscramble these words to make sense of them!

1. NERSFID

2. BGOBLE

3. NVCIAGR KUSNPMPI

4. CNNOIEEP

5. ILGFEAO

6. EVERS

7. LIUSOEDIC

8. EASBN

9. EPPLA BLOECRB

10. TSEAF

11. YRGAV

12. MUUANT RBEZEE

13. OEFLETVRS

14. EFAL IEPL

15. RNCBSRAREIE

thanksgiving jokes

1. Why did the cranberry turn red?
2. What was the scarecrow's favorite fruit?
3. Why can't you take a turkey to church?
4. What always comes at the end of thanksgiving?
5. What do you call a turkey on the run?
6. What do you get when you drop a pumpkin?
7. What is Dracula's all-time favorite holiday?
8. What do you get when you cross a Pilgrim with a cracker?
9. Why was the thanksgiving dinner so expensive?
10. How did the Pilgrims bring their cows to America?

Knock knock.
Who's there?
Pumpkin.
Pumpkin who?

Knock knock.
Who's there?
Pumpkin.
Pumpkin who?

Knock knock.
Who's there?
Pumpkin.
Pumpkin who?

Knock knock.
Who's there?
Orange.
Orange who?

Orange you glad
I didn't say
pumpkin again?

Knock, knock.
Who's there?
Lettuce.
Lettuce who?

Lettuce in, it's cold
out here!

Knock, knock. Who's
there? Norma Lee.
Norma Lee who?

Norma Lee, I don't eat
meat, so I'll have the
mashed potatoes.

1. Because it saw the turkey dressing! 2. Straw-berries! 3. They use fowl language 4. The letter G!
5. Fast food! 6. Squash! 7. Fangsgiving 8. A Pil-graham 9. It had 24 carrots 10. On the
Moooooo-Flower

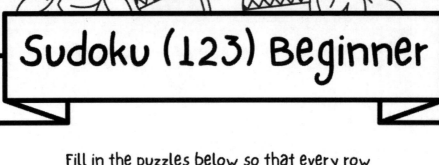

Sudoku (123) Beginner

Fill in the puzzles below so that every row
across, column down and 2x2 box includes
the numbers 1 to 4.

Puzzle #1

1	3	2	
4	2	1	
	1		2
2	4		

Puzzle #2

		2	4
2			1
3			2
		1	

Puzzle #3

3	4	2	
1		3	4

Puzzle #4

	1		
		4	1
	2		
	4	1	

Puzzle #5

2			3
3	4		2
4		3	
1	3	2	4

Puzzle #6

			3
1	3		
2			

Cryptogram Puzzles

Crack the code!
Find the most common letters like 'E' and 'T' and match them with known words. Look for patterns and repeated letters. Use trial and error to substitute different letters until the message is clear.
Keep going until the secret message is revealed!

Cryptogram Puzzle #1

Clue: The meaning of this important holiday!

A	B	C	D	E	F	G	H	I	J	K	L	M	N	O	P	Q	R	S	T	U	V	W	X	Y	Z

```
    A     S          S   A
I L N Y T E S H O H Y S   H E   N
```

```
          S S
I H W C   R Z   I R S C I L C D Y C E E
```

```
A            A
N Y B   S D N I H I P B C
```

Cryptogram Puzzle #2

Clue: Important holiday food!

A	B	C	D	E	F	G	H	I	J	K	L	M	N	O	P	Q	R	S	T	U	V	W	X	Y	Z

```
              A       S
A H B D S O   G Q M   R A H K K I Q Z
```

```
A         A       S
G B S   A N G Q D R Z I V I Q Z
```

```
                A             S
M I Q Q S B   K G V X B I A S R
```

Crossword #2

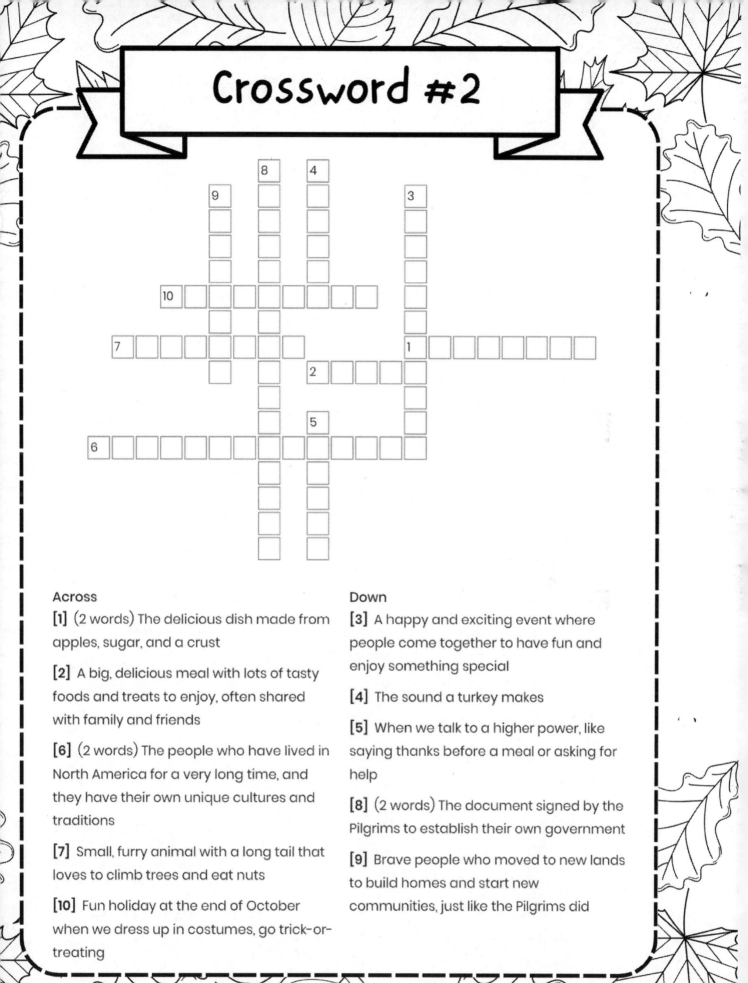

Across

[1] (2 words) The delicious dish made from apples, sugar, and a crust

[2] A big, delicious meal with lots of tasty foods and treats to enjoy, often shared with family and friends

[6] (2 words) The people who have lived in North America for a very long time, and they have their own unique cultures and traditions

[7] Small, furry animal with a long tail that loves to climb trees and eat nuts

[10] Fun holiday at the end of October when we dress up in costumes, go trick-or-treating

Down

[3] A happy and exciting event where people come together to have fun and enjoy something special

[4] The sound a turkey makes

[5] When we talk to a higher power, like saying thanks before a meal or asking for help

[8] (2 words) The document signed by the Pilgrims to establish their own government

[9] Brave people who moved to new lands to build homes and start new communities, just like the Pilgrims did

Word Search #2

Fall

```
E Q S I A U T U M N L E A V E S Q W Y M
S Y J C O R N M A Z E G X N X H T K J F
H A R V E S T M O O N Z Y L O G H M U A
T X U I O H A R V E S T G A W F A R A L
H Q H H A Y R I D E S H M V S A N V P L
A F B A O T M W B O Q I I N T L K P P I
N P J C L O J K P A E Z R P X L S S L N
K X U G O L Q O Q N S O G R X C G C E G
S S L M M O O C N N C X M Q E O I A P L
G T P H P C L W V A N J F A N L V R I E
I K K M E K R B E C J N N W A O I E C A
V B B L B C I W R E I C Y Z E R N C K V
I A I O F P Q N E E N G A V H S G R I E
N U D S N Z T U S W E A T E R S P O N S
G M I Z W F X T K P F Z C T N M A W G Y
V H O U C M I D N W I B E F J I R S V R
C J L X T D B R T L I C T Q S L A W B Q
Z A R M B S U Q E X P P E S C I D E R R
Y W S O U P S E A S O N C W R I E D D S
X S X H A P P G M F A L L F O L I A G E
```

ACORNS   APPLE PICKING   AUTUMN LEAVES
BONFIRES   CIDER   COOL BREEZE
CORN MAZE   FALL COLORS   FALL FOLIAGE
FALLING LEAVES   HALLOWEEN   HARVEST
HARVEST MOON   HAYRIDES   PUMPKIN SPICE
SCARECROWS   SOUP SEASON   SWEATERS
THANKSGIVING   THANKSGIVING PARADE

Maze #2

Copy the Picture

Use the grid to copy the picture.
Copying one square at a time might be easier.
Be careful when counting the squares!

	1	2	3	4	5	6	7
a							
b							
c							
d							
e							
f							
g							
h							
i							
j							
k							
l							

	1	2	3	4	5	6	7
a							
b							
c							
d							
e							
f							
g							
h							
i							
j							
k							
l							

tic-tac-toe

Player _____   Player _____
Score _____   Score _____

Word Scramble #2

Let's unscramble these words to
make sense of them!

1.   IRADHYE

2.   PUTMYLOH OCKR

3.   BIEROFN

4.   UDATTEGRI

5.   LWAFYMOER

6.   EADSMH TASEOTOP

7.   AELPP EDIRC

8.   LRBESSUS SUROTPS

9.   ALCAREM PLPSAE

10. NASRCO

11. MEEORNVB

12. BFTOLLOA

13. EEASLV

14. PUARICOOCN

15. TUYKER

16. ERAGDANSRPNT

17. NWE RLODW

18. PEPLA IIPGNCK

Sudoku (123)
Intermediate

Fill in the puzzles below so that every row across,
column down and 3x3 box includes the numbers 1 to 9.

Puzzle #1

		7	3	6		4	5	1
1		3	5				6	
			1	4	7		8	
	1		2					8
6	9	5			3	7		4
8	7		4	9			3	
			6	3		8	4	9
4	2	8		5		6		
	3		7	8	4	2	1	5

Puzzle #2

9	7		8	5	6	1	3	4
4		8	2	7		6	5	9
	5		9	1		2	8	7
				9				
6			3	4	7		1	
1	3	9	6		2	4		
	2	3		6			9	1
			7	2				
5				3	8	7	2	

Puzzle #3

3	4		7	5		9		
9	7			2			4	5
5			4	3	9	7	1	8
		9		6	4			
		7				5		
	5	4	2	8	7	1		
4	9	3			8	2		7
8	2		9		5		3	1
		5		4	2	6	8	

Puzzle #4

	7	8			4		3	1
		2		8			7	5
5	6		7	3	1			
8	1		5	2		3	6	
					7	2		
3	2		4	6		7	1	9
			6	9		5		
4			7	5	8			
					3			

Word Search #3

Festive Food

```
E H Q N B U T T E R N U T S Q U A S H B
S E B H E L G U C O R N B R E A D U G O
T L T X I B H R B E D D S U A W B C M H
U B A R L T J M E T L G C Y L J E R T C
F D M P Y Y G N E N P H V W Q D S M R R
F B P V P D G X I I N V I U G N A G Q A
I R Y G F L H P F O N B C S R B S E M N
N U M I Y P E F E V Q T E S J E A P A B
G S S B G Y U P E C S X L A O X U C S E
D S P L A T P F I G A L F T N O M O H R
M E H E S C H U W E O N A I S S R R E R
X L P T L E Y V M R Q T P N P C O N D Y
B S Z G S T R Z R P O I I I C I A U P S
C S L R M W U E E P K K V Q E C S C O A
M P V A L F N R T Y P I B L I A T O T U
I R A V B N N E K M X B N K T Z H P A C
E O F Y I J E Y U E B S F P N N A I T E
I U U D J W K P Y N Y N U G I C M A O K
T T B V S K I G R A V Y Q W O E O Z E L
O S R O A S T E D V E G E T A B L E S X
```

APPLE PIE   BRUSSELS SPROUTS   BUTTERNUT SQUASH
CORNBREAD   CORNUCOPIA   CRANBERRY SAUCE
DINNER ROLLS   GIBLET GRAVY   GRAVY
GREEN BEANS   MASHED POTATOES   PECAN PIE
PUMPKIN PIE   PUMPKIN SOUP   ROAST HAM
ROASTED VEGETABLES   STUFFING   SWEET POTATOES
TURKEY

Maze #3

Crossword #3

Across

[2] The different ways that people live, with their own traditions, foods, and celebrations that make them unique.

[4] The ship that brought the Pilgrims to America

[6] (2 words) A mix of spices like cinnamon and nutmeg that makes things like pumpkin pie and lattes taste extra delicious

[7] (2 words) A fun race or run held on Thanksgiving Day where people dress up like turkeys and run together for fun and fitness

[10] Horn of _____ also called a cornucopia, is a special horn-shaped basket filled with all sorts of delicious fruits and vegetables

Down

[1] Special horn-shaped basket filled with all sorts of delicious fruits and vegetables, like a horn of plenty

[3] The month of Canadian Thanksgiving

[5] What colorful things fall from trees in the autumn

[8] A long, narrow boat that you paddle with oars, and it's great for exploring calm waters like lakes and rivers

[9] A big bird with delicious meat, and it's often the star of the Thanksgiving dinner table

Copy the Picture

Use the grid to copy the picture.
Copying one square at a time might be easier.
Be careful when counting the squares!

thanksgiving Story Starter

Complete the thanksgiving story!

"Okay, everyone, deep breaths. We may have a little turkey trouble on our hands, but we can handle it," I announced, trying to keep my composure as the culinary chaos unfolded in the kitchen.

Amid the clatter and confusion, the turkey, a feathery fellow named tom, flapped his wings with enthusiasm and chimed in, "Don't worry, folks! I've got a trick or two up my feathers that might just save thanksgiving dinner. Who's ready for a little turkey magic?"

tic-tac-toe

Player _____   Player _____
Score _____   Score _____

Word Scramble #3

Let's unscramble these words to make sense of them!

1. PEAML SRUYP

2. UTUNAM

3. SSLTONOCI

4. RYBEARCRN AUECS

5. LECABRTEE

6. ETEAWSR EHARTWE

7. OSHIWBNE

8. RMPIGLI

9. GAHINGNC SCROOL

10. ALPEP EPI

11. UHASSQ

12. EAPML ELEVAS

13. UPPNMIK APTCH

14. WROCCEASR

15. UQRELSRI

16. GKHNANTVISGI

17. EVATHSR

18. AECTTAUHMSSSS

thanksgiving Jokes

1. What did the turkey say to the computer?
2. What kind of cars would pilgrims drive today?
3. What do you get when a turkey lays an egg on a hill?
4. What did the baby corn say to mama corn?
5. Why did the turkey cross the road?
6. What do you call a pretty pumpkin?
7. Where did they take the Mayflower when it was sick?
8. What is a turkey's favorite dessert?
9. What's the most musical part of a turkey?
10. What do you use to make thanksgiving bread?

Knock, knock.
Who's there?
Butter.
Butter who?

Butter open up because I've got
a lot of thanksgiving jokes!

Knock, knock.
Who's there?
Waddle.
Waddle who?

Waddle you do with all
those leftovers?

1. Google, Google! 2. Plymouth 3. An eggroll 4. Where's pop-corn? 5. It was the chicken's day off 6. Gourd-geous 7. The nearest doc 8. Peach gobbler! 9. The drumstick 10. May flour

Cryptogram Puzzles

Crack the code!
Find the most common letters like 'E' and 'T' and match them with known words. Look for patterns and repeated letters. Use trial and error to substitute different letters until the message is clear.
Keep going until the secret message is revealed!

.

Cryptogram Puzzle #3

Clue: The first Thanksgiving!

A	B	C	D	E	F	G	H	I	J	K	L	M	N	O	P	Q	R	S	T	U	V	W	X	Y	Z

[ ][ ][ ][ ][ ][ ][S][ ] [A][ ][ ] [ ][A][ ][ ][ ][ ]
P C S W U C Z O   D Y T   Y D R C G K

[A][ ][ ][ ][ ][A][ ][S] [S][A][ ][ ][ ] [A]
D Z K U C Q D Y O   O M D U K T   D

[ ][A][ ][ ][S][ ] [ ][ ][A S][ ]
M D U G K O R   B K D O R

Cryptogram Puzzle #4

Clue: It's about the people who join this holiday!

A	B	C	D	E	F	G	H	I	J	K	L	M	N	O	P	Q	R	S	T	U	V	W	X	Y	Z

[ ][A][ ][ ][ ][ ] [A][ ][ ] [ ][ ][ ][ ][ ][ ][S]
A O Z B L X   O C Y   A H B F C Y J

[ ][ ][ ][ ] [ ][ ][ ][ ][ ][ ][ ] [ ][ ]
N D Z F   I D G F I E F H   I D

[ ][ ][ ][ ][ ][ ][A][ ]
N F L F M H O I F

[ ][ ][ ][ ][A][ ][S][ ][ ][ ][ ]
I E O C K J G B R B C G

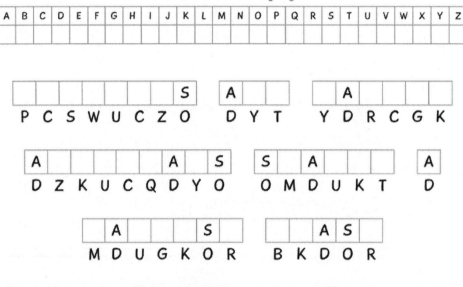

Sudoku (123) Expert

Fill in the puzzles below so that every row across,
column down and 3x3 box includes the numbers 1 to 9.

Puzzle #1

8			2	3	4		1	
2	1			5	9	4		
	5	7		8	1	2		
						6	2	3
9			3	7				
			8		6		4	
	2				8			4
6						3		
1		4						6

Puzzle #2

			2		7	4		1
		4			6			
9		2	4		8			
4	3	7			9			8
2		5	3	8	1	7	6	4
8							5	9
3		8	1		4	9		
			7					3
7	4				6			

Puzzle #3

		4	7			6		
2	9	5			6	8	4	
7		1			9			
			1			2	9	
		9					6	5
		3			4		8	1
6			9			1	3	
	3	7			1	4	5	
	4			6				8

Puzzle #4

2			6			8	9	5
6		5		2				
9		1	4		5			8
4			3			2	7	
3	2		7	4				5
		6						
		2				7		1
	9	3		6		5		
	1				7			

Word Search #4

travel

```
T P P L O N G D I S T A N C E S N L U D
R J M N E S P A F F W I W E Z T B C S E
B O C O R R S R O A I R P O R T S M T P
A X A C Q O B R B S P R C K W N A O R A
R T R D O O T I L T I E U U W J N L A R
C R R B T S W V O Q Z U H L C B E S I T
B A E U G R Z A E X Q N G I G V O S N U
P V N P T C I L P H W T F G A X T N T R
P E T T K N Q P W B Y F F R C I W W R E
A L A R H X B P S J A R T G S R A L A E
D S L A O W B U A R C Y S I S G Y U V U
V N S V T T X W T C A J V N F J U G E E
E A C E E F K S Y D K Y O I A I F G L N
N C P L L Y L U I Z L I E K D Q E A A A
T K O D S T Q L W I N X N C N Y C G H S
U S I E T G O N M U G K V G F R G E N T
R I O L A H G A E L P P T F D G K G H Z
E X F A Y Q F R X W Z D I U I A A Y U I
O E I Y S T W O R O A D M A P S Q D E W
V I N S T E T R A V E L E X P E N S E S
```

ADVENTURE	AIRPORTS	ARRIVAL
CAR RENTALS	DEPARTURE	FAMILY VISITS
HOLIDAY TRAVEL	HOTEL STAYS	LONG DISTANCES
LUGGAGE	PACKING	REUNIONS
ROAD MAPS	ROAD TRIPS	TRAFFIC JAMS
TRAIN TRAVEL	TRAVEL DELAYS	TRAVEL EXPENSES
TRAVEL SNACKS		

Maze #4

Crossword #4

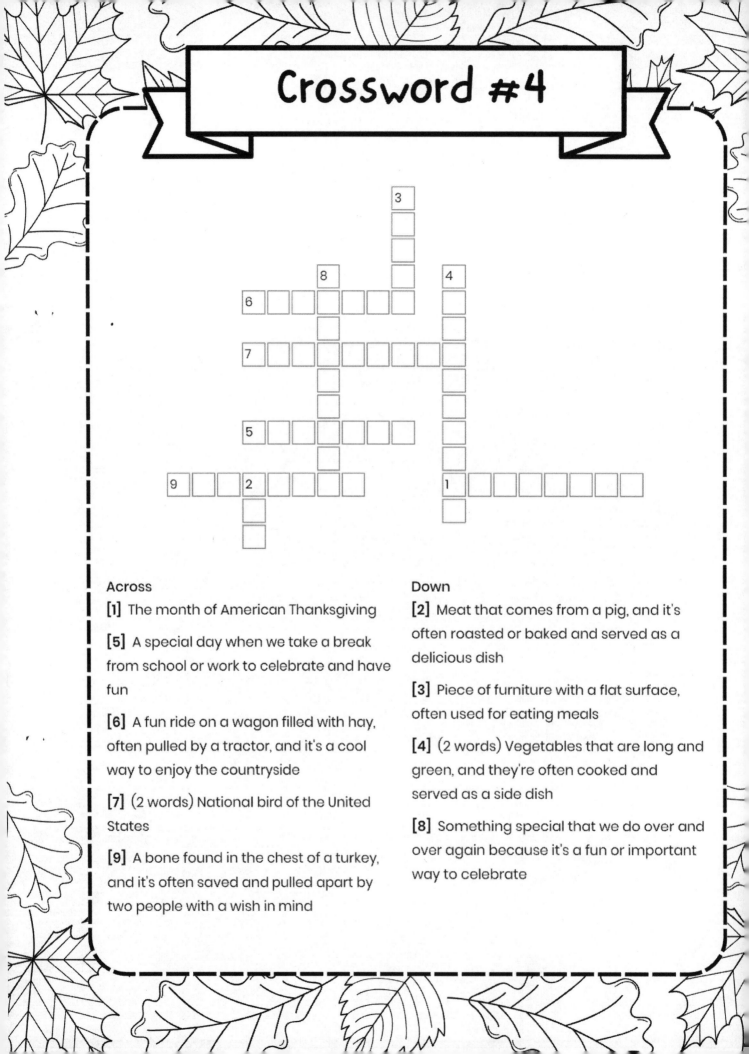

Across

[1] The month of American Thanksgiving

[5] A special day when we take a break from school or work to celebrate and have fun

[6] A fun ride on a wagon filled with hay, often pulled by a tractor, and it's a cool way to enjoy the countryside

[7] (2 words) National bird of the United States

[9] A bone found in the chest of a turkey, and it's often saved and pulled apart by two people with a wish in mind

Down

[2] Meat that comes from a pig, and it's often roasted or baked and served as a delicious dish

[3] Piece of furniture with a flat surface, often used for eating meals

[4] (2 words) Vegetables that are long and green, and they're often cooked and served as a side dish

[8] Something special that we do over and over again because it's a fun or important way to celebrate

Draw the Other Half

Use the grid to draw the other half of the picture.

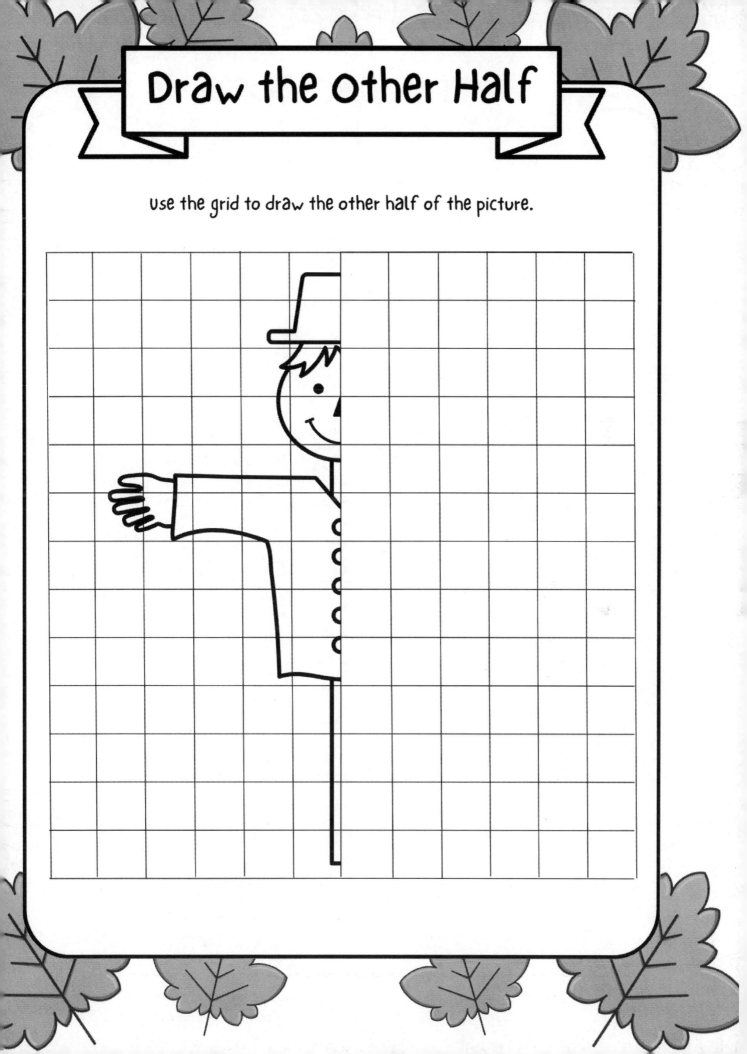

tic-tac-toe

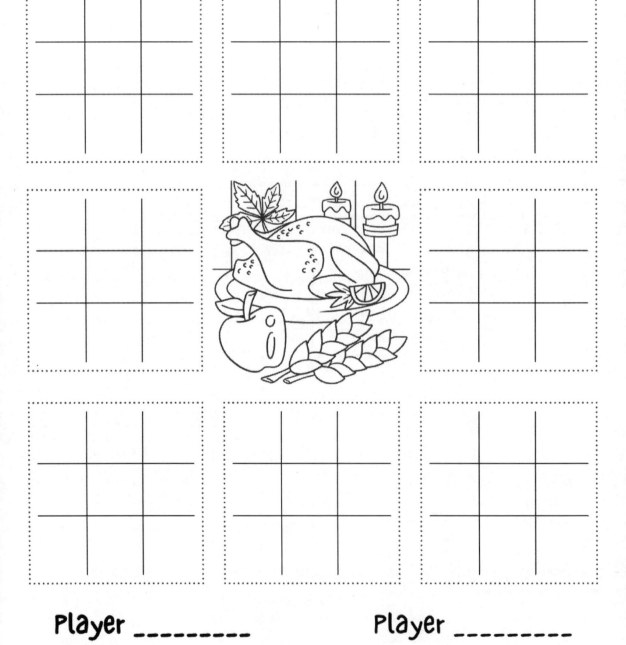

Player _____   Player _____

Score _____   Score _____

Double Puzzle #1

Unscramble the jumbled words to make sense! Once you've solved it, you can unveil the secret word at the bottom of the puzzle.

ESETW PAETTOSO

[ ][ ][15][ ][ ] [6][ ][ ][ ][ ][ ][ ][ ]

TARSO

[ ][ ][ ][ ][ ]

UAOSNTQ

[ ][ ][7][ ][12][ ][ ]

LDIOYAH

[ ][ ][ ][11][ ][ ][1]

TFERALGU

[ ][ ][ ][ ][ ][ ][ ][ ]

DINNIA

[ ][ ][ ][ ][ ][ ]

SAHAKTCY

[ ][ ][5][ ][ ][ ][ ][10]

CKPUTOL

[13][ ][ ][ ][ ][ ][ ]

AERCV

[ ][ ][ ][ ][ ]

TAENIV AEAICMRN

[ ][ ][ ][ ][ ][ ][ ] [ ][4][ ][ ][ ][ ][ ][ ]

IPMKPNU

[9][2][3][ ][ ][14][ ]

OYMHUTPL

[ ][ ][ ][8][ ][ ][ ][ ]

[1][2][3][4][5] [6][7][8][9][10][11][12] [13][14][15]

Sudoku (abc) Beginner

Fill in the puzzles below so that every row across, column down and 2x2 box includes the letters A to D.

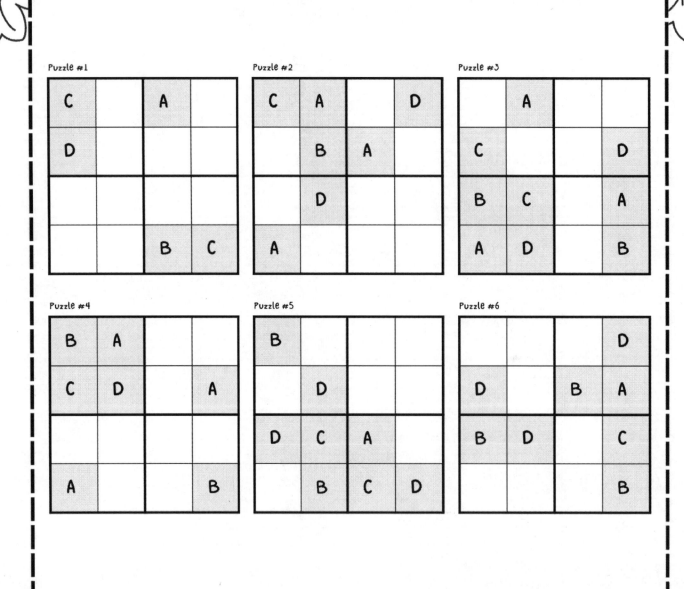

Puzzle #1

C		A	
D			
		B	C

Puzzle #2

C	A		D
	B	A	
	D		
A			

Puzzle #3

		A		
C			D
	B	C		A
	A	D		B

Puzzle #4

B	A		
C	D		A
A			B

Puzzle #5

B			
	D		
D	C	A	
	B	C	D

Puzzle #6

			D
D		B	A
B	D		C
			B

Crossword #5

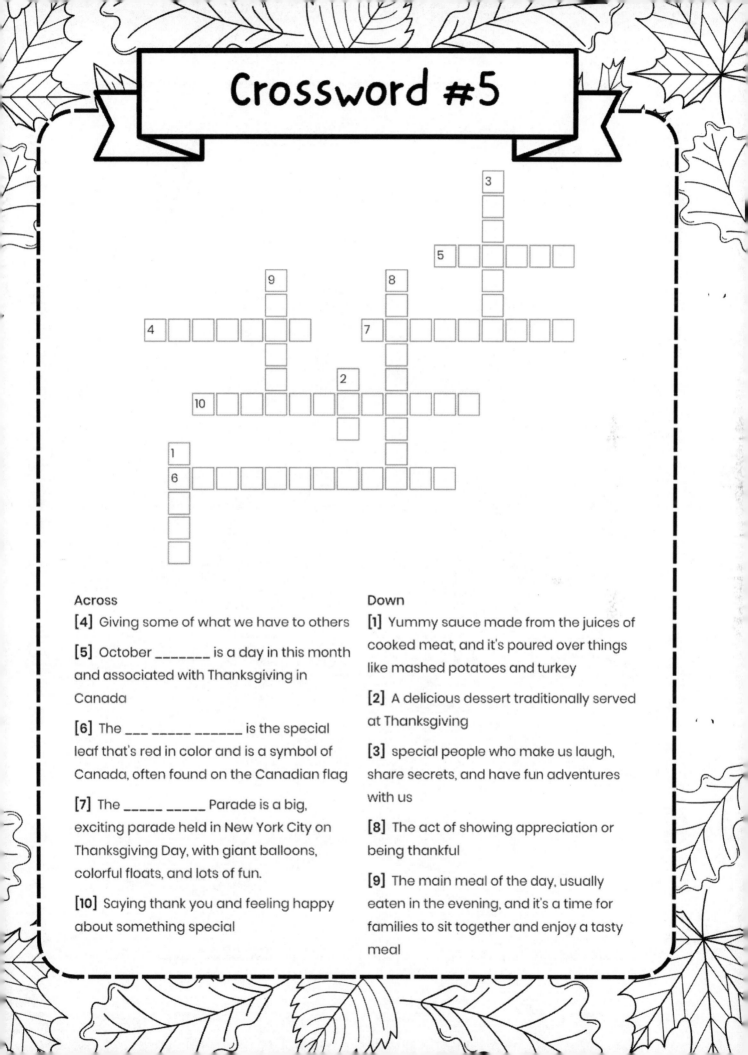

Across

[4] Giving some of what we have to others

[5] October _____ is a day in this month and associated with Thanksgiving in Canada

[6] The ___ _____ _____ is the special leaf that's red in color and is a symbol of Canada, often found on the Canadian flag

[7] The _____ _____ Parade is a big, exciting parade held in New York City on Thanksgiving Day, with giant balloons, colorful floats, and lots of fun.

[10] Saying thank you and feeling happy about something special

Down

[1] Yummy sauce made from the juices of cooked meat, and it's poured over things like mashed potatoes and turkey

[2] A delicious dessert traditionally served at Thanksgiving

[3] special people who make us laugh, share secrets, and have fun adventures with us

[8] The act of showing appreciation or being thankful

[9] The main meal of the day, usually eaten in the evening, and it's a time for families to sit together and enjoy a tasty meal

Word Search #5

Gratitude

```
P Y T E A N O I T C E L F E R H F V N F
T I X G Y T I S O R E N E G R Q Z B P X
H S N R Q B T H A N K F U L N E S S L Z
A S M A K I E E Y N P S G V K D Y R H M
N E Y T Z H I X U V E R M F X Y T N X T
K N O E W Y V I R G R A C E L H G J H C
S I C F A G O A P P R E C I A T I O N G
G P L U G K X T V L T S M J R S G S D G
I P O L N I W X K P C A Z K H R M E O S
V A V V T C V Y A U F I M A A F G K N K
I H E V S B H I Q V Z S R T R F F T A K
N P G V E G P Y N M W I I I D C U L B W
G Y D G V E E A L G N T E N C I P U U E
P M M A R L T W M G U N D Z K U J A N L
R W C L A P S F Y D D S E I Y P D W D W
A A Y G H K D A E S X L R Q M Q P J A B
Y Z Z T N E T I N M A D H A B T T C N W
E N O A T B M I D K I N D N E S S U C D
R Y H X B L E S S I N G S E A O L B E V
U T O L X Q O H E A L T H L S F S F S D
```

ABUNDANCE	APPRECIATION	BLESSINGS
FAMILY	FRIENDS	GENEROSITY
GIVING	GRACE	GRATEFUL
GRATITUDE	HAPPINESS	HARVEST
HEALTH	KINDNESS	LOVE
REFLECTION	SHARING	THANKFULNESS
THANKS	THANKSGIVING PRAYER	

Maze #5

Draw the Other Half

Use the grid to draw the other half of the picture.

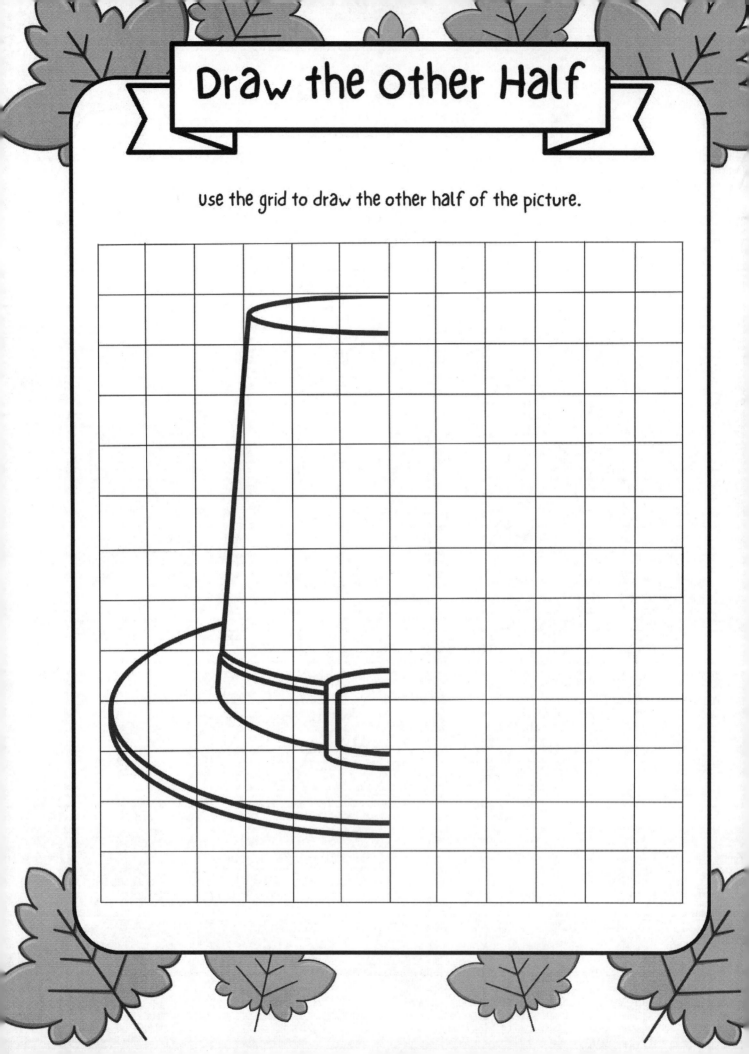

tic-tac-toe

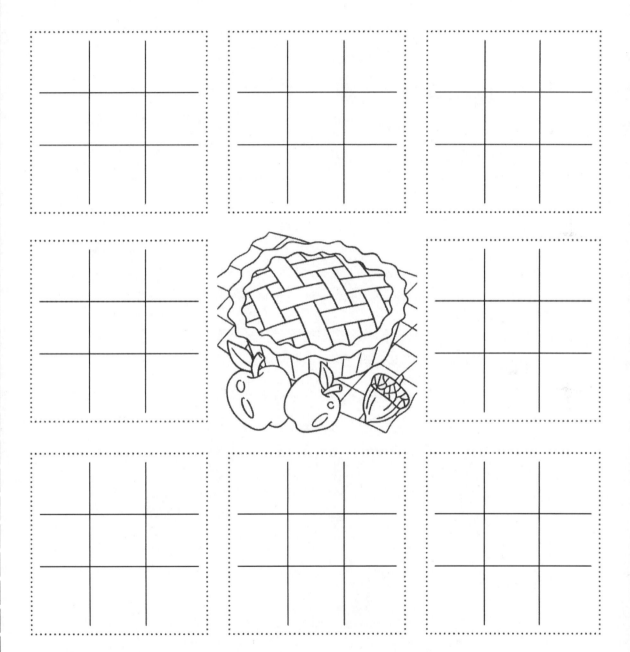

Player _____   Player _____

Score _____   Score _____

unscramble the jumbled words to make sense! Once you've solved it, you can unveil the secret word at the bottom of the puzzle.

RSCROTA

AENCO — 13

EERICP

ISBGSNELS — 12

NPECA EIP — 10

MCEDRAE NCOR — 8 4

KPUMINP SECIP — 6 9

IMFAYL — 3

OETREHGT — 2

ABAMHR CNNLLIO — 7

GTSANVIIKHNG — 11 14

UGDTITEAR — 5

J | | | | | — 1 2 3 4 5 6

| | | | | | | | — 7 8 9 10 11 12 13 14

Sudoku (abc)
Intermediate

Fill in the puzzles below so that every row across,
column down and 3x3 box includes the letters A to I.

Puzzle #1

		F		A	H			B
G	B			D				
	H	E	B					
B				C	D		G	
	G				I	H		
		D						
		E	I		H		A	
D	I	B		H			C	E
	E	A	F			G		

Puzzle #2

					B		C	
		H			H	I	A		F
I		D		A		B	E	
E		C	B		D		H	
H				A				
	A		H			D		G
A	I				C	F	B	
	E			G	H			I
	H	B					E	

Puzzle #3

C			E		A	D		
F		G			E	A		
	E	A	B					
A		H	F	B		I		
	G			D				
E		D		I		C		
H		F	G	E			A	
D				B	F		G	
		D			H	B		

Puzzle #4

		I	C				H	
		C	B					I
H	B		A		E			
B	G	A	E		F	I	D	H
		E	I	D		G	F	A
D	I	F		G				
F	C			E			I	
A				I	C			
	G	D		A				F

Crossword #6

Across

[2] The sport often watched on TV during Thanksgiving

[4] (2 words) The place where the Pilgrims first landed in America

[5] The colorful band worn around a turkey's neck

[8] (2 words) The American holiday celebrated on the fourth Thursday of November

[10] (2 words) A sweet, yummy liquid made from trees, and it's delicious on pancakes and waffles

Down

[1] _____ sauce is a sweet and tangy sauce made from red berries, and it's a yummy part of Thanksgiving dinner

[3] People who have always lived in a certain place, and they have their own special traditions and ways of life

[6] The act of saying thanks before a meal

[7] (2 words) The autumn festival that celebrates the harvest

[9] The Native American tribe that helped the Pilgrims survive

Word Search #6

Decorations

```
C Y H A R V E S T D E C O R A L U A G Z
J T U X I I N D I A N C O R N P R J V B
T T U R K E Y D E C O R J N M B D T Z A
Q Q O P Q C R M K O C A N D L E S A P U
Y O E I O G F H V R B C D Y M Y Y B F N
U N M L Z J I C V N N O N B W O P L A B
S W P G D B N L U S R Z F B J K X E L H
L C A R P I N E C O N E S G D Y B C L O
F E U I H N D Y G P W Z H L N Z U L F R
B N T M K H Y Y W C P R U D A B N O L N
M T U H G F S O S I M L E A Q D T T O O
H E M A A H R C B S Z P A A Z Y I H W F
V R N T L C W G X A J A U C T I N A E P
T P L S E I D O R H N E T M E H G D R L
D I E R M N U U P F L N J N P C I E S E
L E A O S S I R O H B A E F B K A W Y N
Q C V G F V O D T J S C R R R O I R N T
S E E A U Q Q S G X O D D T S E Q N D Y
X L S K W E M C O R N U C O P I A O S S
H O B Q Z U J H P U U B Z V D O Y Q C K
```

ACORNS	AUTUMN LEAVES	BANNERS
BUNTING	CANDLES	CENTERPIECE
CORNUCOPIA	FALL FLOWERS	GOURDS
HARVEST DECOR	HORN OF PLENTY	INDIAN CORN
PILGRIM HATS	PINE CONES	PLACE CARDS
PUMPKINS	SCARECROW	TABLECLOTH
TURKEY DECOR	WREATH	

Maze #6

Draw the Other Half

Use the grid to draw the other half of the picture.

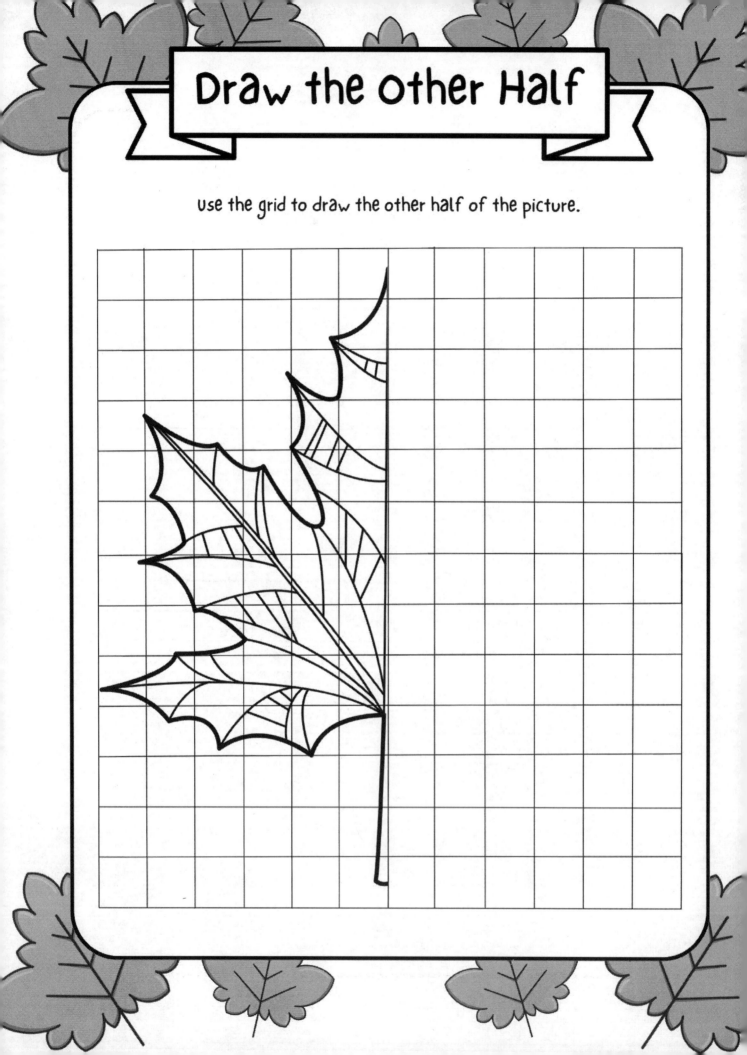

thanksgiving Story Starter

Complete the thanksgiving story!

"Grandma, why are they saying there might not be a thanksgiving parade this year?"
I asked, my eyes wide with concern as we passed by a bulletin board filled with the
sad notice.

My grandmother, a twinkle in her eye and a heart full of determination, bent down
and whispered, "Well, dear, I believe it's high time we do something about it. What do
you say we come up with a plan to save the parade and bring a little joy back to our
town?"

_____

_____

_____

_____

_____

_____

_____

_____

_____

_____

_____

_____

_____

_____

tic-tac-toe

Player _____   Player _____

Score _____   Score _____

Double Puzzle #3

unscramble the jumbled words to make sense! Once you've solved it, you can unveil the secret word at the bottom of the puzzle.

NMREEBVO ☐☐☐☐☐☐☐☐
8

DAAERP ☐☐☐☐☐☐

EAOVGY ☐☐☐☐☐☐
3 7

REIGTNHGA ☐☐☐☐☐☐☐☐☐
1

RGCAE ☐☐☐☐☐

HYENO AHM ☐☐☐☐☐ ☐☐☐

EEDTSSR ☐☐☐☐☐☐☐
10 4

ASTRO REUYKT ☐☐☐☐☐ ☐☐☐☐☐☐
9

OWRHPSI ☐☐☐☐☐☐☐
6

MAYFIL ☐☐☐☐☐☐

CCOAPRINUO ☐☐☐☐☐☐☐☐☐☐
2

ALLOFTOB ☐☐☐☐☐☐☐☐
5

☐☐☐☐ ☐☐☐☐☐☐
1 2 3 4 5 6 7 8 9 10

Would You Rather?

Here are some fun and challenging Thanksgiving questions to ask your friends and family.

Would you rather have to say "gobble" at the end of every sentence during thanksgiving dinner
or
have to perform a turkey dance before every bite?

Would you rather attend a thanksgiving dinner where everyone speaks in rhyme
or
a dinner where everyone communicates in charades?

Would you rather travel back in time to spend a day as a Pilgrim aboard the Mayflower
or
as a Native American welcoming the Pilgrims to the New World?

Would you rather always feel too full
or
a little hungry?

Would you rather always smell like turkey
or
like gravy?

Would you rather eat an entire pumpkin pie
or
drink the whole gravy boat?

Would you rather get $100 dollars for every slice of pie you ate
or
get $1,000 for eating no thanksgiving food at all?

Would you rather eat thanksgiving leftovers fo an entire year
or
never eat thanksgiving food again?

Would you rather wear a pilgrim hat to school for all of November
or
eat thanksgiving food for every day of November?

Cryptogram Puzzles

Crack the code!
Find the most common letters like 'E' and 'T' and match them with known words. Look for patterns and repeated letters. Use trial and error to substitute different letters until the message is clear.
Keep going until the secret message is revealed!

Cryptogram Puzzle #5

Clue: We watch these during the holiday!

A	B	C	D	E	F	G	H	I	J	K	L	M	N	O	P	Q	R	S	T	U	V	W	X	Y	Z

_ A _ A _ S   _ A _   _ _ _ _ _ A _
Q P T P N O I   P Y N   B G G Z E P X X

_ A _ _ S   _ A _   _ _ _ _ _ _ _ _ _
K P M O I   P N N   O S A L Z O M O Y Z

_ _   _ _ _ _   _ _ _ _ _ A _
Z G   Z H O   H G X L N P C

Cryptogram Puzzle #6

Clue: The thing people do best during Thanksgiving!

A	B	C	D	E	F	G	H	I	J	K	L	M	N	O	P	Q	R	S	T	U	V	W	X	Y	Z

S _ _ _ _ _ _ _   _ _   _ A _ _   _ S
F U G K K D E C   I H   K P W L   D F

_ _   _ _ _ _ _ A _   _ S
I H   R V Q D B P H

S _ _ _ _ _ _ _ _ _
F G S L O S V Z L O

Sudoku (abc) Expert

Fill in the puzzles below so that every row across,
column down and 3x3 box includes the letters A to I.

Puzzle #1

A		E	H	D			B	
	B	D	F	E	G		H	I
		F	A		B			
	I							B
G			B	H	D		F	
D		B					C	H
			I			C		E
E					F	B		G
			E			H	A	F

Puzzle #2

C	G			D			H	A
	A		G		B	C		
I		F			C		E	G
E	F							
	I		B	G		H	F	
	H	D			I		C	
H		G	E	I				
E			C					H
	C	I		B	H	G	A	E

Puzzle #3

	H			E		G		
	I	F	H				E	
		E	A		C	H	B	
D		I	B	F	H			
		H			I	B	F	
F				C				H
H			I					C
		C	B		I			
I			E	H	G			

Puzzle #4

						B	H	I
A	B	C	D				G	F
	H		B	F	G		A	D
	I		H	A		F	G	
E	D			G				E
		E	H	D		F		B
		I		E				G
F					I	D		
	B			D			I	C

Answers

Crossword Solutions

Thanksgiving Crossword #1

[1↓] Corn
[2↓] Abundance
[3↓] Stuffing
[4↓] Orange
[5↓] Family
[6→] Scarecrow
[7→] Autumn
[8→] Pilgrims
[9↓] Squanto
[10→] Pumpkin

Thanksgiving Crossword #2

[1→] Applepie
[2→] Feast
[3↓] Celebration
[4↓] Gobble
[5↓] Prayer
[6→] Nativeamerican ·
[7→] Squirrel
[8↓] Mayflowercompact
[9↓] Settlers
[10→] Halloween

Thanksgiving Crossword #3

[1↓] Cornucopia
[2→] Cultures
[3↓] October
[4→] Mayflower
[5↓] Leaves
[6→] Pumpkinspice
[7→] Turkeytrot
[8↓] Canoe
[9↓] Turkey
[10→] Plenty

Thanksgiving Crossword #5

[1↓] Gravy
[2↓] Pie
[3↓] Friends
[4→] Sharing
[5→] Twelve
[6→] Redmapleleaf
[7→] Macy'sday
[8↓] Gratitude
[9↓] Dinner
[10→] Appreciation

Thanksgiving Crossword #4

[1→] November
[2↓] Ham
[3↓] Table
[4↓] Greenbeans
[5→] Holiday
[6→] Hayride
[7→] Baldeagle
[8↓] Tradition
[9→] Wishbone

Thanksgiving Crossword #6

[1↓] Cranberry
[2→] Football
[3↓] Indigenous
[4→] Plymouthrock
[5→] Wattle
[6↓] Grace
[7↓] Harvestfestival
[8→] Thanksgivingday
[9↓] Wampanoag
[10→] Maplesyrup

Wordsearch Solutions

Thanksgiving Wordsearch #1 - Autumn Colors

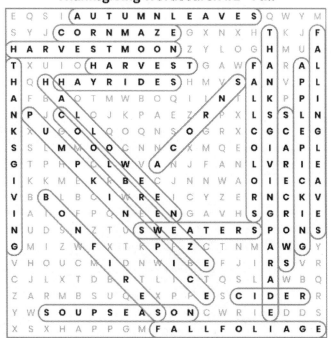

Thanksgiving Wordsearch #2 - Fall

Thanksgiving Wordsearch #3 - Food

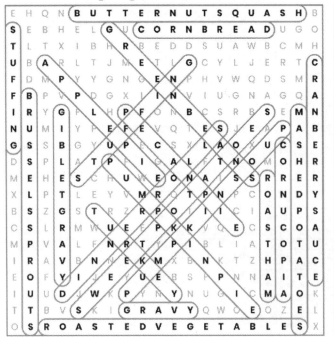

Thanksgiving Wordsearch #4 - Travel

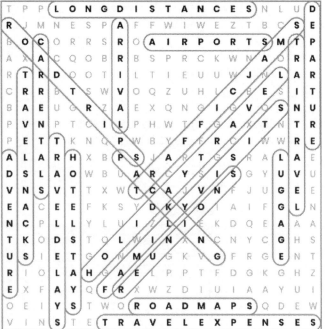

Word Search Solutions

Thanksgiving Wordsearch #5 - Gratitude

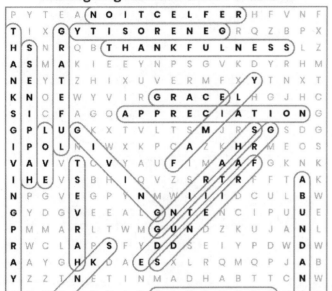

Thanksgiving Wordsearch #6 - Decorations

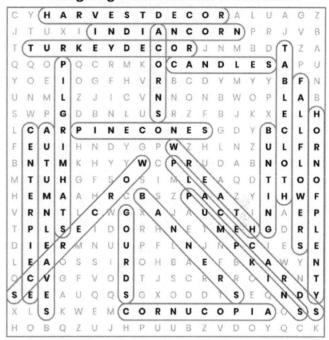

Maze Solutions

Maze #1

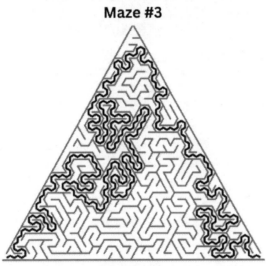

Maze #2

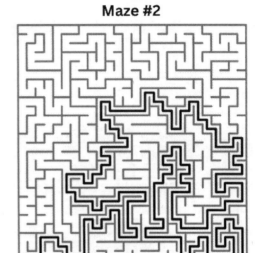

Maze #3

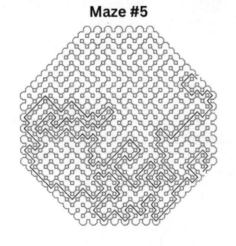

Maze #4

Maze #5

Maze #6

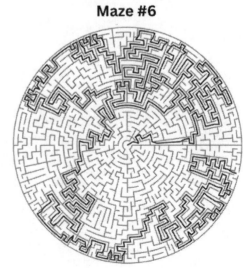

Word Scramble Solutions

Word Scramble #1

1. NERSFID — F R I E N D S
2. BGOBLE — G O B B L E
3. NVCIAGR KUSNPMPI — C A R V I N G   P U M P K I N S
4. CNNOIEEP — P I N E C O N E
5. ILGFEAO — F O L I A G E
6. EVERS — S E R V E
7. LIUSOEDIC — D E L I C I O U S
8. EASBN — B E A N S
9. EPPLA BLOECRB — A P P L E   C O B B L E R
10. TSEAF — F E A S T
11. YRGAV — G R A V Y
12. MUUANT RBEZEE — A U T U M N   B R E E Z E
13. OEFLETVRS — L E F T O V E R S
14. EFAL IEPL — L E A F   P I L E
15. RNCBSRAREIE — C R A N B E R R I E S

Word Scramble #2

1. IRADHYE — H A Y R I D E
2. PUTMYLOH OCKR — P L Y M O U T H   R O C K
3. BIEROFN — B O N F I R E
4. UDATTEGRI — G R A T I T U D E
5. LWAFYMOER — M A Y F L O W E R
6. EADSMH TASEOTOP — M A S H E D   P O T A T O E S
7. AELPP EDIRC — A P P L E   C I D E R
8. LRBESSUS SUROTPS — B R U S S E L S   S P R O U T S
9. ALCAREM PLPSAE — C A R A M E L   A P P L E S
10. NASRCO — A C O R N S
11. MEEORNVB — N O V E M B E R
12. BFTOLLOA — F O O T B A L L
13. EEASLV — L E A V E S
14. PUARICOOCN — C O R N U C O P I A
15. TUYKER — T U R K E Y
16. ERAGDANSRPNT — G R A N D P A R E N T S
17. NWE RLODW — N E W   W O R L D
18. PEPLA IIPGNCK — A P P L E   P I C K I N G

Word Scramble #3

1. PEAML SRUYP — M A P L E   S Y R U P
2. UTUNAM — A U T U M N
3. SSLTONOCI — C O L O N I S T S
4. RYBEARCRN AUECS — C R A N B E R R Y   S A U C E
5. LECABRTEE — C E L E B R A T E
6. ETEAWSR EHARTWE — S W E A T E R   W E A T H E R
7. OSHIWBNE — W I S H B O N E
8. RMPIGLI — P I L G R I M
9. GAHINGNC SCROOL — C H A N G I N G   C O L O R S
10. ALPEP EPI — A P P L E   P I E
11. UHASSQ — S Q U A S H
12. EAPML ELEVAS — M A P L E   L E A V E S
13. UPPNMIK APTCH — P U M P K I N   P A T C H
14. WROCCEASR — S C A R E C R O W
15. UQRELSRI — S Q U I R R E L
16. GKHNANTVISGI — T H A N K S G I V I N G
17. EVATHSR — H A R V E S T
18. AECTTAUHMSSSS — M A S S A C H U S E T T S

Double Puzzle Solutions

Double Puzzle #1

ESETW PAETTOSO — S W E E T   P O T A T O E S

TARSO — R O A S T

UAOSNTQ — S Q U A N T O

LDIOYAH — H O L I D A Y

TFERALGU — G R A T E F U L

DINNIA — I N D I A N

SAHAKTCY — H A Y S T A C K

CKPUTOL — P O T L U C K

AERCV — C A R V E

TAENIV AEAICMRN — N A T I V E   A M E R I C A N

IPMKPNU — P U M P K I N

OYMHUTPL — P L Y M O U T H

Y U M M Y   P U M P K I N   P I E
1 2 3 4 5   6 7 8 9 10 11 12   13 14 15

Double Puzzle #2

RSCROTA — C A R R O T S

AENCO — C A N O E

EERICP — R E C I P E

ISBGSNELS — B L E S S I N G S

NPECA EIP — P E C A N   P I E

MCEDRAE NCOR — C R E A M E D   C O R N

KPUMINP SECIP — P U M P K I N   S P I C E

IMFAYL — F A M I L Y

OETREHGT — T O G E T H E R

AABAMHR CNNLLIO — A B R A H A M   L I N C O L N

GTSANVIIKHNG — T H A N K S G I V I N G

UGDTITEAR — G R A T I T U D E

J O Y O U S   O C C A S I O N
1 2 3 4 5 6   7 8 9 10 11 12 13 14

Double Puzzle #3

NMREEBVO — N O V E M B E R

DAAERP — P A R A D E

EAOVGY — V O Y A G E

REIGTNHGA — G A T H E R I N G

RGCAE — G R A C E

HYENO AHM — H O N E Y   H A M

EEDTSSR — D E S S E R T

ASTRO REUYKT — R O A S T   T U R K E Y

OWRHPSI — W O R S H I P

MAYFIL — F A M I L Y

CCOAPRINUO — C O R N U C O P I A

ALLOFTOB — F O O T B A L L

G I V E   T H A N K S
1 2 3 4   5 6 7 8 9 10

Cryptogram Solutions

Cryptogram Puzzle #1

A	B	C	D	E	F	G	H	I	J	K	L	M	N	O	P	Q	R	S	T	U	V	W	X	Y	Z
N	A	F	B	C	Z	S	L	H	V	T	M	W	Y	R	K	X	D	E	I	P	O	G	U	J	Q

T H A N K S G I V I N G   I S   A
I L N Y T E S H O H Y S   H E   N

T I M E   O F   T O G E T H E R N E S S
I H W C   R Z   I R S C I L C D Y C E E

A N D   G R A T I T U D E
N Y B   S D N I H I P B C

Cryptogram Puzzle #2

A	B	C	D	E	F	G	H	I	J	K	L	M	N	O	P	Q	R	S	T	U	V	W	X	Y	Z
G	P	W	M	S	K	Z	N	I	J	D	T	C	Q	X	F	E	B	R	A	H	V	L	Y	O	U

T U R K E Y   A N D   S T U F F I N G
A H B D S O   G Q M   R A H K K I Q Z

A R E   T H A N K S G I V I N G
G B S   A N G Q D R Z I V I Q Z

D I N N E R   F A V O R I T E S
M I Q Q S B   K G V X B I A S R

Cryptogram Puzzle #3

A	B	C	D	E	F	G	H	I	J	K	L	M	N	O	P	Q	R	S	T	U	V	W	X	Y	Z
D	F	Q	T	K	B	W	M	C	E	X	S	Z	Y	J	P	L	U	O	R	N	G	A	I	H	V

P I L G R I M S   A N D   N A T I V E
P C S W U C Z O   D Y T   Y D R C G K

A M E R I C A N S   S H A R E D   A
D Z K U C Q D Y O   O M D U K T   D

H A R V E S T   F E A S T
M D U G K O R   B K D O R

Cryptogram Solutions

Cryptogram Puzzle #4

A	B	C	D	E	F	G	H	I	J	K	L	M	N	O	P	Q	R	S	T	U	V	W	X	Y	Z
O	M	N	Y	F	A	G	E	B	S	K	L	Z	C	D	V	U	H	J	I	T	R	W	Q	X	P

FAMILY   **AND**   **FRIENDS**
A O Z B L X   O C Y   A H B F C Y J

COME   **TOGETHER**   **TO**
N D Z F   I D G F I E F H   I D

CELEBRATE
N F L F M H O I F

THANKSGIVING
I E O C K J G B R B C G

Cryptogram Puzzle #5

A	B	C	D	E	F	G	H	I	J	K	L	M	N	O	P	Q	R	S	T	U	V	W	X	Y	Z
P	E	A	N	O	B	K	H	L	F	J	X	M	Y	G	Q	W	T	I	Z	V	U	R	S	C	D

PARADES   **AND**   **FOOTBALL**
Q P T P N O I   P Y N   B G G Z E P X X

GAMES   **ADD**   **EXCITEMENT**
K P M O I   P N N   O S A L Z O M O Y Z

TO   **THE**   **HOLIDAY**
Z G   Z H O   H G X L N P C

Cryptogram Puzzle #6

A	B	C	D	E	F	G	H	I	J	K	L	M	N	O	P	Q	R	S	T	U	V	W	X	Y	Z
P	A	W	B	L	K	C	R	D	T	M	Q	I	E	V	S	Y	O	F	U	G	X	Z	J	H	N

STUFFING   **MY**   **FACE**   **IS**
F U G K K D E C   I H   K P W L   D F

MY   **HOLIDAY**
I H   R V Q D B P H

SUPERPOWER
F G S L O S V Z L O

Sudoku (123) Solutions

Beginner Solutions

Puzzle #1

1	3	2	4
4	2	1	3
3	1	4	2
2	4	3	1

Puzzle #2

1	3	2	4
2	4	3	1
3	1	4	2
4	2	1	3

Puzzle #3

3	4	2	1
2	1	4	3
1	2	3	4
4	3	1	2

Puzzle #4

4	1	2	3
2	3	4	1
1	2	3	4
3	4	1	2

Puzzle #5

2	1	4	3
3	4	1	2
4	2	3	1
1	3	2	4

Puzzle #6

4	2	1	3
1	3	4	2
3	4	2	1
2	1	3	4

Intermediate Solutions

Puzzle #1

2	8	7	3	6	9	4	5	1
1	4	3	5	2	8	9	6	7
5	6	9	1	4	7	3	8	2
3	1	4	2	7	6	5	9	8
6	9	5	8	1	3	7	2	4
8	7	2	4	9	5	1	3	6
7	5	1	6	3	2	8	4	9
4	2	8	9	5	1	6	7	3
9	3	6	7	8	4	2	1	5

Puzzle #2

9	7	2	8	5	6	1	3	4
4	1	8	2	7	3	6	5	9
3	5	6	9	1	4	2	8	7
2	4	7	5	9	1	3	6	8
6	8	5	3	4	7	9	1	2
1	3	9	6	8	2	4	7	5
7	2	3	4	6	5	8	9	1
8	6	1	7	2	9	5	4	3
5	9	4	1	3	8	7	2	6

Puzzle #3

3	4	8	7	5	1	9	2	6
9	7	1	8	2	6	3	4	5
5	6	2	4	3	9	7	1	8
1	3	9	5	6	4	8	7	2
2	8	7	1	9	3	5	6	4
6	5	4	2	8	7	1	9	3
4	9	3	6	1	8	2	5	7
8	2	6	9	7	5	4	3	1
7	1	5	3	4	2	6	8	9

Puzzle #4

9	7	8	2	5	4	6	3	1
1	3	2	9	8	6	4	7	5
5	6	4	7	3	1	9	8	2
8	1	7	5	2	9	3	6	4
6	4	9	3	1	7	2	5	8
3	2	5	4	6	8	7	1	9
7	8	1	6	9	2	5	4	3
4	9	3	1	7	5	8	2	6
2	5	6	8	4	3	1	9	7

Sudoku (123) Solutions

Expert Solutions

Puzzle #1

8	6	9	2	3	4	7	1	5
2	1	3	7	5	9	4	6	8
4	5	7	6	8	1	2	3	9
7	8	1	4	9	5	6	2	3
9	4	6	3	7	2	5	8	1
5	3	2	8	1	6	9	4	7
3	2	5	9	6	8	1	7	4
6	9	8	1	4	7	3	5	2
1	7	4	5	2	3	8	9	6

Puzzle #2

5	6	3	2	9	7	4	8	1
1	8	4	5	3	6	2	9	7
9	7	2	4	1	8	5	3	6
4	3	7	6	5	9	1	2	8
2	9	5	3	8	1	7	6	4
8	1	6	7	4	2	3	5	9
3	5	8	1	6	4	9	7	2
6	2	1	9	7	5	8	4	3
7	4	9	8	2	3	6	1	5

Puzzle #3

3	8	4	7	5	2	6	1	9
2	9	5	3	1	6	8	4	7
7	6	1	4	8	9	5	2	3
8	7	6	1	3	5	2	9	4
4	1	9	2	7	8	3	6	5
5	2	3	6	9	4	7	8	1
6	5	8	9	4	7	1	3	2
9	3	7	8	2	1	4	5	6
1	4	2	5	6	3	9	7	8

Puzzle #4

2	4	7	6	1	8	9	5	3
6	8	5	9	2	3	4	1	7
9	3	1	4	7	5	6	2	8
4	5	9	3	8	1	2	7	6
3	2	8	7	4	6	1	9	5
1	7	6	5	9	2	8	3	4
5	6	2	8	3	9	7	4	1
7	9	3	1	6	4	5	8	2
8	1	4	2	5	7	3	6	9

Sudoku (ABC) Solutions

Beginner Solutions

Puzzle #1

C	B	A	D
D	A	C	B
B	C	D	A
A	D	B	C

Puzzle #2

C	A	B	D
D	B	A	C
B	D	C	A
A	C	D	B

Puzzle #3

D	A	B	C
C	B	A	D
B	C	D	A
A	D	C	B

Puzzle #4

B	A	C	D
C	D	B	A
D	B	A	C
A	C	D	B

Puzzle #5

B	A	D	C
C	D	B	A
D	C	A	B
A	B	C	D

Puzzle #6

A	B	C	D
D	C	B	A
B	D	A	C
C	A	D	B

Intermediate Solutions

Puzzle #1

I	D	F	C	A	H	G	E	B
G	B	C	I	D	E	A	F	H
A	H	E	B	F	G	C	I	D
B	F	I	H	E	C	D	A	G
E	G	D	A	B	F	I	H	C
C	A	H	D	G	I	E	B	F
F	C	G	E	I	B	H	D	A
D	I	B	G	H	A	F	C	E
H	E	A	F	C	D	B	G	I

Puzzle #2

G	A	F	H	E	B	I	C	D
B	E	H	D	C	I	A	G	F
I	C	D	G	A	F	B	E	H
E	G	C	B	I	D	F	H	A
H	D	I	F	G	A	E	B	C
F	B	A	C	H	E	D	I	G
A	I	G	E	D	H	C	F	B
C	F	E	A	B	G	H	D	I
D	H	B	I	F	C	G	A	E

Puzzle #3

C	H	B	E	F	A	D	G	I
F	D	G	H	C	I	E	A	B
I	E	A	B	G	D	C	H	F
A	C	H	F	B	E	G	I	D
B	G	I	C	D	H	A	F	E
E	F	D	A	I	G	B	C	H
H	B	F	G	E	C	I	D	A
D	A	C	I	H	B	F	E	G
G	I	E	D	A	F	H	B	C

Puzzle #4

E	A	I	C	G	D	F	H	B
G	F	C	B	H	E	D	A	I
H	B	D	A	F	I	E	G	C
B	G	A	E	C	F	I	D	H
C	H	E	I	D	B	G	F	A
D	I	F	H	A	G	C	B	E
F	C	B	G	E	H	A	I	D
A	D	H	F	I	C	B	E	G
I	E	G	D	B	A	H	C	F

Sudoku (ABC) Solutions

Expert Solutions

Puzzle #1

A	G	E	H	D	I	F	B	C
C	B	D	F	E	G	A	H	I
I	H	F	A	C	B	G	E	D
H	I	A	C	F	E	D	G	B
G	E	C	B	H	D	I	F	A
D	F	B	G	I	A	E	C	H
F	A	G	I	B	H	C	D	E
E	C	H	D	A	F	B	I	G
B	D	I	E	G	C	H	A	F

Puzzle #2

C	G	E	I	D	F	B	H	A
D	A	H	G	E	B	C	I	F
I	B	F	H	A	C	D	E	G
E	F	B	C	H	D	A	G	I
A	I	C	B	G	E	H	F	D
G	H	D	A	F	I	E	C	B
H	D	G	E	I	A	F	B	C
B	E	A	F	C	G	I	D	H
F	C	I	D	B	H	G	A	E

Puzzle #3

B	H	C	F	D	E	A	G	I
A	I	F	H	G	B	C	E	D
G	D	E	A	I	C	H	B	F
D	A	I	B	F	H	G	C	E
C	G	H	D	E	I	B	F	A
F	E	B	G	C	A	D	I	H
H	B	G	I	A	F	E	D	C
E	F	A	C	B	D	I	H	G
I	C	D	E	H	G	F	A	B

Puzzle #4

G	F	D	C	A	E	B	H	I
A	B	C	D	I	H	E	G	F
I	H	E	B	F	G	C	A	D
B	I	H	A	C	F	G	D	E
E	D	F	I	G	B	A	C	H
C	G	A	E	H	D	F	I	B
D	A	I	F	E	C	H	B	G
F	C	G	H	B	I	D	E	A
H	E	B	G	D	A	I	F	C

Made in United States
Orlando, FL
05 November 2024

53511267R00043